GREAT TRAINERS
MAKE IT HAPPEN!

BEN OLSON

ISBN: 1-4196-8114-1
ISBN-13: 9781419681141

Visit www.booksurge.com to order additional copies.

Acknowledgements

Professional Guidance

The following individuals have provided me with mentorship, coaching, training, guidance, and inspiration. Knowing each of you has been a privilege, and I am extremely grateful for the opportunity to have worked with you over the years.

Aylwin Lewis, Pat Evans, Doug McCallum, Sue Weber, Tom Cagle, Richard Gnepper, Tammy Zurek, Agustin Garcia, Alberta Morrison, and Dave Pettigrew.

Family and Friends

I am so grateful to my family and friends for providing me a constant bridge of strength, love and support. Not a day goes by that I do not thank the heavens for each of you!

Shelby Olson, Lauren Olson, Cara Olson, Melissa Sherman, Martin Olson, Charlie and Ronnie Krahn, Ali Amir, Alice Massie, Diane Massie, Lori Caccippio, and Professor Daniel C. Spaniel

Editing and Illustrations

A big thank you to *Lauren Olson,* whose keen editing eye and playful illustrations helped this book take shape! Thanks for doing <u>so much more</u> than just crossing the t's and dotting the i's!

Dedication

To Shelby

*"Faith is believing in something,
even when common sense
tells you not to."*

Thanks for believing in me.

Please send your questions or
comments to:

ben.olson@cptrainer.net

For more *Great Trainer* information
visit my website:

www.cptrainer.net

Preface
Who Should Read This Book?

Experienced Trainers:
Enhance Your Training Sessions With Style!

Training is one job where experience alone does not make one "great." Truly great trainers are constantly on the look-out for new ideas, methods, and techniques that will, first and foremost, enhance the learning experience of their students, and also make them a better trainer in the process. If you are an experienced trainer, you will find many helpful and new ideas in this book that you can use in the classroom tomorrow, and many more that you can chew on in the weeks ahead. Chapter 3 will be of special interest to experienced trainers, as it poses the question: *Are you an "Instructor" or a "Tour Guide" to learning?*

New Trainers: You Are Not Alone!

Being new in the training field, you will inherently have the tendency to focus your preparation efforts on yourself. I know, I've been there, done that. In fact, you will read about my first training experience and how one student's comment became my wake-up call to change. It happened to me, but it does not have to happen to you! This book provides specific and easy-to-execute examples that, when utilized, will make any rookie trainer look like a seasoned pro in just one day! In addition, you will have a foundation to formulate ideas for future classes that will put you on the road to continuous training improvement!

Other Professionals and Occasional Trainers: Help Is Here!

If you are one of the thousands of professionals who only occasionally receive the assignment to conduct classroom-style training, *and dread every minute of it,* this little book will save you! A quick and easy read, <u>*Great Trainers Make It Happen!*</u> will provide you with methods that I guarantee will energize your students. It will motivate them to learn, and help you become more comfortable in the role of "trainer." Plus, the results will make your boss proud!

"You can't <u>make</u> people do anything.
The most you can hope for is to show them how to
do it, and then say, follow me."
– Isaac Stern
Master Violinist **1920-2001**

Follow me to learn how to become a Great Trainer!

Table of Contents

Introduction
From The Trenches: My Story

Long ago, and not so far away, a much younger Ben Olson had just completed 2 weeks of a train-the-trainer course that consisted of role-playing, guided practice, and a lot of study. As I accepted my certificate of completion, I was filled with excitement, ready to teach my first class solo.

The Preparation

I spent an entire week planning for the "Big Day." I reviewed the material several times, cover to cover. I practiced my dialog on my wife, and when she could not stand any more, I made my dog listen to me. I took the advice of my training instructor and videotaped myself to look for those common body language distractions such as: Don't put your hands in your pockets, don't pick your nose, that type of thing. Also, to listen not only to <u>what</u> I was saying, but <u>how</u> I was saying it - through voice tone, inflection, and all the rest. For that week, the world really did revolve around <u>me</u>.

Sleepless In Chicago

I did not sleep much the night before my first class, because I was so excited (actually, *really* nervous!) but by the time class began the next morning, I honestly felt that I could teach just about anything to anyone. I believed I was 100% prepared! What I didn't know, was that I was about to learn a hard lesson that would change my teaching style forever.

The Delivery

The first half of class was awesome. I mean, <u>I was awesome</u>, flying through the material, cracking occasional jokes, and establishing my credibility as the topical expert extraordinaire. The words flowed from my mouth like a Montana river on a windswept spring day. I noticed several students taking copious notes. One young man in particular seemed to hang on my every word. From my vantage point, I could see his pencil flying over his note pad through out the morning session. I remember thinking, "Wow, he must be learning a <u>ton</u> of things from my presentation!" In fact, I felt I was doing so well that some disappointment set in when it came time to break for lunch, but you know, people do have to eat. Reluctantly, I announced the lunch break and the students slowly filtered out of the room. And then it happened.

The Truth Comes Out

The student who was sitting in the back row…the young man that was taking notes like a maniac…approached me on his way out the door. "Mr. Olson, I'm really enjoying watching you talk," he said. Not totally sure what he was getting at, I smiled and replied, "Why, thank you! Tell me, what have you learned so far?" I was fully expecting accolades about my outstanding teaching ability. His answer stunned me. "Well, I haven't learned much of anything new so far, but I did want to present you with this. I've been working on it all morning and I think it turned out really well, don't you?" He handed me a page of what I thought were his class notes. Instead, I discovered that what he had been so diligently penciling was a caricature of me! This is a copy of the actual picture. Not a bad likeness of me at the time!

A Hard Lesson, But One Worth Learning!

After all these years, I do not recall this young man's name. I hope he reads this book and contacts me so that I can not only give him credit for his artwork, but also to thank him. I have saved this picture because it serves as a reminder about the valuable lesson I learned that day. The lesson was:

Trainers, It's Not About You;
It's All About The Learner!

The mistake I made on that day long ago is a mistake still made by many trainers today.

They focus all their energy in the wrong place; on themselves. Inexperienced trainers are most likely to fall into the trap of focusing on *their* material, *their* communication style, *their* presentation needs, just as I did. But Great Trainers do it differently and so much better! Great Trainers take the exact opposite approach when planning for a training session because they understand the fundamental rule of effective training: *Always focus on the learner!* They begin planning for their class by focusing on the needs of the student <u>first</u>. As we will learn in Chapter 1, that process begins with creating an inviting physical learning environment.

My Guarantee

It's likely that you will see yourself in more than one of these chapters. As trainers, when we make mistakes we need to raise our hand and be held accountable. But sometimes "stuff happens." At one time or another, we all have felt the blow of budget cuts, material shortages, and glares from hostile students. Things happen. You can't avoid it. However, you will see in the following chapters that if you plan and prepare with the focus being on the needs of the learner, you will have structured the classroom experience in such a positive way that I guarantee it will make a difference in your professional life, and therefore, also in the livelihood of your students. Assuming ownership, taking action, and enhancing the learning experience in the classroom is what this book is all about.

Practice These Techniques and Become One of The Great Ones!

As with all learning, training, and self-development, taking action doesn't just make a difference; taking action makes all the difference. It is one thing to read this book, but quite another to put these methods into action. And that is my challenge to you as we begin. There is indeed a huge difference between being a good trainer and a Great Trainer, and I can only assume that the reason you are reading this book is because you want to become a Great Trainer. If you use the information outlined in this book, you will be well on your way to becoming the Great Trainer you have always wanted to be, because although *good trainers* may know these methods, *Great Trainers* are the ones who make them happen!

Chapter 1
Create an Inviting Physical Learning Environment

Plan Your Training To Be Learner-Focused From The Start!

The goal of training is universal in that, regardless of the topic, the final expectation is to change behavior back on the job. Period! So the real question is: How do you, as a trainer, develop the session to become so effective and so inspiring that the participants will not only apply what they learn, but will actually be *excited* to learn more? Spitting out information "lecture style" to students, expecting them to apply their new knowledge with few or no questions asked, just doesn't cut it with the adult learner. Today's learner has certain expectations that must be met, and these expectations are usually developed days before they step into the classroom. Understanding this, Great Trainers employ certain fundamentals as they plan their training sessions. Mediocre trainers don't understand the objectives or methods of learner-focused training, and they literally ruin the learning experience for the student before the first bell rings. Here is a real life example of an experience I had with such a trainer.

Tales From The Dark Side

I attended a 2-day food safety seminar. The purpose of the seminar was to educate and license the participants in safe food handling practices. Pretty important stuff, considering all the foodborne illness outbreaks we continue to hear about in the news, many caused by the food handlers themselves. However, my expectations were shattered before the class even began. The "training room" was located in the basement of a budget hotel. No refreshments were served, not even water. Remember, this was a 2-day class! Tables were in disrepair, and the chairs were plastic and very uncomfortable. (Try sitting 8 hours a day, for two days, in a plastic chair!) Lighting was dim at best. The carpeting was heavily soiled, and a light scent of mildew permeated the room. Only one unisex washroom was available, and it was so close to the training area that you could hear, let's just say "sounds," every time it was used. Can you say "distraction"?

And What About the Participants?

Did they talk about how they would take the food safety training back to their jobs and share the information with others? Were they excited to use their new knowledge to make food safer for customers? Of course not! They were so focused on the distracting conditions of the learning environment - it's all they could talk about! In this case, the instructor was clearly focused on herself (or her pocketbook) and gave no consideration to the learning environment of the students.

What Great Trainers Do

A Great Trainer, realizing the importance of retention and on-the-job application, would ensure the training environment was comfortable and conducive to learning, discussion, and participation. These fundamentals in themselves cause the learner to be more receptive to the material, increasing retention and the likelihood of accomplishing our primary goal of changing behavior back on the job.

Great Trainers Checklist

Follow these tips to create an inviting learning environment for your students.

Size Matters! The room should be large enough to allow participants ample "elbow" room between seats. Try using round tables, seating 4-5 per table. This arrangement facilitates group discussions. If you structure the training session right, your participants will learn as much from each other as they do from you!

Keep It Bright! Lighting must be adequate. People enjoy bright surroundings. Studies have proven a relationship between light (brightness) and mood alteration. Simply put, bright rooms make people feel good. Good moods equal higher levels of attention and better reception of the material.

Cleanliness Is a Must! Col. Harland Sanders, founder of

Kentucky Fried Chicken, coined the phrase: "Cleanliness is next to godliness." He was right. Make sure your training room is clean. That includes floors, carpets, walls, tables, air vents, and light fixtures.

Serve Refreshments! You don't need to break the bank on this one. Simply having water available with a few snacks is practical, appreciated <u>and</u> expected.

Restroom Requirements! Be sure adequate restroom facilities are available based on the size of the class. As previously discussed, one unisex restroom for 20 people is not adequate!

Check Out Chairs and Tables! They should be in good repair, and chairs must be comfortable. Participants report one <u>of the greatest learning distractions</u> is sitting in an uncomfortable chair for 8 hours.

Comfort = Air Flow and Temperature! Ventilation, heating, and air conditioning are extremely important factors to consider in order to keep your group comfortable and focused on the material. If it is 60 degrees in the room, don't expect anyone to be listening to your instruction or feeling motivated to participate in discussions. They are all too busy thinking up ways to keep warm!

The Bottom Line About The Physical Learning Environment

Keeping participants comfortable in a clean, spacious, well-lit, well-ventilated room with comfortable chairs and refreshments will keep them focused on the topics at hand. And keeping them focused is what leads to learning, retention, and on-the-job application. *Good trainers* may know this, but **Great Trainers make it happen!**

Chapter 2
Create an Inviting Emotional Learning Environment

The Emotional Tone Is Set In Stone

Equally as important as the physical learning environment is the *emotional tone* the trainer will establish in the classroom. Notice I used the words "will establish," because it will happen. Whether you take specific actions or do nothing at all, you <u>will</u> establish an emotional tone. The moment a participant enters the training room *"The emotional tone is set in stone"* for the remainder of the class. All the senses are at work during that critical entrance moment: sight, smell, audio and physical. The brain is sifting through this information, and in a nanosecond (well, ok, maybe a minute or two), it creates an emotional response. In other words, the brain tells the heart "Here's how you should *feel* about this class." Many trainers see the emotional tone as "fluff and stuff," underestimating the power of the heart as it relates to the emotional response to our surroundings. Great Trainers would agree, this is a substantial miscalculation that can quickly lead to participant "shut down" right from the very beginning of class.

Capture The Heart! But How?

As an *instructor*, you can cram a lot of information into a person's brain, and after class, they will return to work and spill out portions of what they learned, just as you *instructed* them to do. But a Great Trainer who captures the heart of their students will notice the participants' increased levels of attention, retention, and application, all of which equate to better long-term results. You can do this by making people feel welcome in your classroom. Include them in the learning experience instead of making them feel like a spectator in a classroom. Solicit ideas, lead discussions, and not only allow, but encourage, students to ask the really tough questions. Finally, as Great Trainers, we must always be approachable. People need to feel as though there is someone they can turn to for help when they really need it. Who better to "be there" during trying times than the person who taught the skill set? Consider yourself to be an on-going resource for the students. <u>Great Trainers understand that when class is over</u>, <u>the real work is just beginning</u>. Ask yourself: What do your students feel when they walk into your training room? What do you do to capture their heart? What do you do to set a positive emotional tone in your classroom?

Tales From The Dark Side: Revisited

Let's look at the same seminar we discussed in Chapter 1 from the view of the emotional tone that was established by the trainer. Class was scheduled to begin at 8:30 a.m. I arrived at 8:10 a.m. and the person at the hotel front desk directed me to the basement meeting room. As I entered the room, I noticed five other students had also arrived early. We sat silently (in those darn plastic chairs), staring at a whiteboard that contained notes from a previous, unrelated meeting. No visuals, no sounds, no books, nothing to do or say, and worse, no trainer present. To break the uncomfortable silence and boredom, occasionally someone would comment about the musty smell in the room, or the unusually warm weather of the day, but for the most part, we all simply sat in silence. The trainer walked in 10 minutes prior to the class start time. She did not acknowledge any of the students. In fact, she did not even smile. A young man sitting next to me whispered, "Uh-oh, she looks mad – this won't be pretty!" As other students arrived for class, the trainer failed to greet them as well.

At exactly 8:30 a.m. she stood up and announced her name, gave an extremely detailed description of her qualifications (making it clear this was *all about her*), handed out the workbooks, and began the class – lecture style, of course!

What Was the Emotional Tone Set By This Trainer?
- This will be boring, so settle in for a long day.
- I don't want to be here any more than you do.
- What you need, want, and expect to get from this class is not important to me.
- Don't bother asking questions; just let me get through this material.
- If you get hungry or thirsty - sorry, you're on your own.

The Students React

There is an old saying: *When people <u>show</u> you who they are, believe them!* Through her behavior, this trainer showed us "who she was" and, as her students, we believed her. She didn't care about the quality of the learning environment. The class was indeed boring, the students did not ask any questions, and we were all taken aback that although no snacks or beverages were provided for us, the trainer enjoyed her private stash of goodies <u>as we watched</u>! (Most people would agree that was just plain rude!)

It became painfully obvious that she cared little about the physical learning environment, and through the emotional tone *she* established, it became clear from the very beginning that she did not care about the students either.

Mama, Don't Let Your Babies Grow Up To Be Trainers, Unless...

Frankly, if you see yourself behaving as this trainer did, you would do everyone a favor by finding another line of work. The world has enough trainers and teachers who don't care. We don't need anymore, thank you! On the other hand, if you are beginning to see there is a better way to train, if you believe that establishing a positive physical and emotional learning environment will open the door to enhanced learning, if you really do care about the students that fill your classroom - then please read on!

What Great Trainers Do To Enhance the Physical and Emotional Learning Environment of Their Classroom

Actions always speak louder than words. Realizing this:
- *Great Trainers* understand the importance of creating a welcoming physical and emotional learning environment for their students and they take actions to develop and provide that environment!
- *Great Trainers* talk less, listen more, and display positive behaviors that send a clear message of what students can expect from the learning experience.
- *Great Trainers* know that adults may be complicated creatures, but the adult learning process is not. If students are physically comfortable, made to feel welcome, and remain involved in their learning process, they will have a good training experience. Insist on this type of learning environment for your students.
- *Great Trainers* know that a good training experience equates to higher levels of participation, attention, retention and on-the-job application.
- In other words, Great Trainers go **WACCO** for their students in the classroom!

Great Trainers Create an Inviting Emotional Learning Environment In The Classroom By Going WACCO For Their Students!

Welcome Everyone: Establish a Personal Rapport!

Meet and greet every participant as they enter the room. Making people feel welcome will cause them to be relaxed and feel as though they are actually a "participant" in the training event, not just an "attendee." This also breaks down the trainer/student barrier that may exist in the mind of the student. By the time class begins, students have met the trainer and already feel they know them on a more personal level. By establishing a rapport with students prior to the start of class, they will feel more comfortable asking questions, which will immediately increase the level of participation and attention!

Action: Make Your Classroom Come Alive!

Have some PowerPoint slides running on the screen to give an element of action to the room. These introductory slides can be a combination of class topics, fun quotes, and even cartoons! Next, add some music! A word of caution: be sure your music selection is appropriate for the audience. I suggest purchasing a CD of old TV show theme songs. People enjoy recalling the old shows, and in no time, the room will be buzzing with recollections and stories of favorite actors and episodes. It really gets people talking, helping to put them at ease. As the saying goes, "A relaxed mind is an open mind." In our case, make that open to learning!

Create Curiosity: Get People Wondering About The Topics!

I once attended a training seminar where I noticed two

baskets of potatoes - big Idaho potatoes - placed on a table in the room. I won't give this activity away, but I will tell you it sent an immediate message to people as they walked in to the seminar room; *this class is going to be different!* If you will be using props for certain training activities, have them out on display. Create curiosity and you also create anticipation and interest! (If you want to get the details of the "potato activity," drop me a line. It's a surprising demonstration of "Believing is Achieving.")

Create Color: Add Some Magic To Your Classroom!

Color, Color, Color! It captures and holds our attention, brightens our moods, and makes everything more fun to experience. Add color to your classroom through the use of photographs and posters. Dress up those bland tables by adding colored markers, post-it note cards, name tents and other colorful class materials.

Opportunity: It's There For The Taking!

Being in the position of "trainer," you should understand one thing: classroom leadership is a privilege, one that presents both the trainer and the student with great opportunities. This fact should be a humbling reminder to all of us. When we step in front of a group of people, we have been given both the privilege and the responsibility of leading students through an experience that could very well change their lives by changing and improving the quality of their livelihoods.

Every class you teach is an opportunity for everyone in the room to learn something new. Search out those opportunities by focusing on the needs of the learner.

The Bottom Line About The Emotional Learning Environment

Great Trainers understand that when class is over, the real work is just beginning. Use the **WACCO** process and you will create and manage the emotional learning environment by making the classroom come alive with activity and color before the class begins! This will create a welcoming environment for your students and cause participation to increase, expectations to rise, and attention levels to soar.

Good trainers may know this, but ***Great Trainers* make it happen!**

Next Up: How would you like to become a "Tour Guide" to learning?

Chapter 3
Classroom Leadership – Become a "Tour Guide" to Learning!

Make Your Training Classes Anything <u>But</u> Ordinary!

We should think of our training room environment in the same light that we think about our favorite restaurant. What makes you want to go back? If you examine your memories of your favorite place, you'll likely find a few things that stand out, such as exceptional service, a fun or exciting atmosphere, etc. You are made to feel comfortable and accepted, making the very thought of returning an inviting proposition. Your favorite restaurant is probably anything but "ordinary" to you. If you want students to have a memorable learning experience…if you want them to come back…you must make their training experience anything <u>but</u> ordinary! In this chapter, we'll discuss specific methods that every trainer can use to deliver anything-but-ordinary training, while maintaining the focus on the learner!

True Story: I Needed Help!

I was developing a food safety training program for my company. Next to chemical engineering, food safety training is about as dry a topic as you can find. I was desperately searching for creative ideas to inject into the course. After writing about 50% of the course material, I hit a wall. I could see that my course was not much different than others I had attended. I needed fresh ideas (and fast!) so I signed up to attend a 2-day train-the-trainer course provided by a premier national training company based in Minneapolis, Minnesota. By attending this course, I assumed I would be "taught" methods and techniques that I could use in the course I was writing.

Welcome To a Totally WACCO Learning Environment!

Entering the seminar room that first day was an experience in itself. Colorful materials adorned the participant tables, music was softly playing in the background, and cartoon drawings with words of wisdom flashed on the projection screen. As I found a seat, the trainer approached me, introduced himself and welcomed me to the class. He asked questions about my expectations, and specifically what I needed to take away from the seminar. Sound familiar? The trainer was utilizing the **WACCO** principles discussed in Chapter 2. Finding myself in the position of the learner, I was now very eager to see what he had in store for us *before* the seminar even began!

Meet Your "Tour Guide" to Learning!

As the seminar got underway, he introduced himself and then explained that he would not "instruct" us; rather, he would act as our "tour guide" to learning. As any good tour guide would do, he planned to "show us around" the topics, providing expertise in certain areas. "More importantly," he stated, "I will allow you to wander, explore, discover, and yes, even question the content of the course. As your tour guide, my main responsibility is to ensure you don't get lost during the tour!" Well this sounded mighty intriguing, but I was skeptical. How did he expect us to *learn* anything if we were not *taught*? I decided to keep an open mind and experience for myself what our "tour guide" had to offer.

The Results

Within the first four hours of this seminar, I realized the course I had started was written from the "instructor" point of view. It was all wrong! I decided that I would need to rewrite my entire course from the point of view of the tour guide. To start from scratch seemed like a daunting task, yet I was filled with excitement and anticipation. I simply could not wait to get back to work and use my new knowledge. From a learner's perspective, my tour guide came through as promised!

Are You an "Instructor" or a "Tour Guide"?

I've known plenty of instructors who <u>thought</u> they were tour guides, but their actions didn't back up their words. And I was one of them! How did I change? The same way you can change. First, start by making an honest self-evaluation of your training style and skills. As a trainer, acknowledge who you are vs. who you want to become. Take a close look at the following behavior comparison chart. Circle the behaviors that you need to develop. Which ones will make you a better tour guide?

Behavior Comparison Chart: Instructor vs. Tour Guide

An Instructor Will:	A Tour Guide Will:
Lecture students, allowing little or no discussion of topics, ideas, or opinions.	Facilitate discussion among students to entertain opinions and new ideas.
Tell students what to do, when to do it, what to think, and when to think it.	Show them the way; allow students to come to their own conclusions on how best to use the information learned.
Tell stories to illustrate how best to use the information learned.	Ask students to provide examples of how to best use the information learned in real life settings.
Focus on getting through all of the training material, and finishing on time.	Focus on the learner, ensuring they understand the material, as well as the practical application.
Provide all the options that are available to the students, and allow them to select from that list.	Encourage students to determine and openly discuss options, deciding for themselves.
Believe students should listen to them because they are the topical expert; after all, that's why they are the instructor.	Believe that students should listen to each other because most adults learn best through networking and personal discovery.
Say that classroom leadership is both a privilege and a responsibility, but fail to "walk the talk."	Believe that classroom leadership is both a privilege and a responsibility, and display that belief through their actions everyday.
Follow the timeline of the class and show little flexibility to allow additional Q&A time.	Be approachable, making time to be a resource for students before and after class.
Make copies of the sign-in sheet and tell people to call each other.	Not only encourage networking, but provide a specific method to do so, as part of an established process.

Next Steps

In Chapters 4, 5, and 6, you will find specific methods that are designed to aid in your development as a tour guide to learning. Keep reading, and bring your pencil.

The Bottom Line About Becoming A Tour Guide To Learning

Acting as a tour guide will help you become a more effective trainer, and will cause adult learners to return to the workplace *excited* to put their new knowledge to work. Utilizing tour guide techniques will make your class anything-but-ordinary, causing people to actually look forward to your next event! Finally, remember that classroom leadership is both a privilege and a responsibility; display that belief through your actions every day! *Good trainers* may know this, but **Great Trainers make it happen!**

Great Trainer Mid-Term Review

Let's review what we have learned up to this point. Making students feel comfortable in both their physical and emotional environment is key for a successful classroom experience. The old-school lecture days of instruction are long gone. Today's learner has much higher expectations. They want to interact with the trainer and each other. Allow people the opportunity to socialize, and they will relax. When people feel at ease, they are more open to learning and they are more inclined to participate. And, as we will discuss in Chapter 4, participation is key to the development of ownership in the learning experience.

Key Points to Remember: Chapters 1-3

Chapter 1 – The Physical Learning Environment

Creating an inviting physical environment is the first critical step in the delivery of any successful training session. Keeping participants comfortable in a clean, spacious, well-lit, well-ventilated room with comfortable chairs and refreshments will keep them focused on the topics at hand. And keeping them focused is what leads to learning, retention, and on-the-job application.

Chapter 2 – The Emotional Learning Environment

Equally as important is the <u>emotional tone</u> you establish in your classroom. The moment a participant enters the training room *"The emotional tone is set in stone"* for the remainder of the class. You can create and manage the emotional learning environment by making the classroom come alive with activity and color before the class begins! This will create a welcoming environment for your students and cause participation to increase, expectations to rise, and attention levels to soar.

Chapter 3 – Classroom Leadership–Become a "Tour Guide" to Learning!

Acting as a "tour guide" will help you become a more effective trainer, and will cause adult learners to return to the workplace *excited* to put their new knowledge to work. Utilizing tour guide techniques will make your class anything-but-ordinary, causing people to look forward to your next training event! Finally, remember that classroom leadership is both a privilege and a responsibility; display that belief through your actions very day!

Chapter 4
Participant Ownership

The Trainer-Learner Relationship

Much has been said relating to the responsibility of the trainer in the learning process.

And it's all true. But there is another important side to the relationship between the trainer and the learner. As with all good relationships, the learning process becomes a partnership of sorts; each member relying on the other to do their part to ensure success. For the part of the participant, there are two rules they must keep in mind:

Rule #1: The expectation of the training is that they will take ownership in the learning process and apply their new skills back on the job.

Rule #2: You can't change Rule #1.

However, getting people to take ownership in their learning experience is not always an easy task. In fact, nowadays it is downright challenging. Participant ownership has become another spectator sport in classrooms across the country. Why? I believe there are two main causes.

Caution: Social Commentary Ahead!

First, it's a societal phenomenon. Over the past 30 years we have done a great job of telling our children (today's adult learner) that nothing is their fault (even when it is), everyone is a winner (even when they are not), and if you don't have what you need, someone else is at fault for not providing it to you (conveniently removing them from all responsibility). Through a complex mix-match of both social and family values, many of today's adult learners believe that it is the trainer's sole responsibility to teach, which will <u>cause</u> them to learn. If it doesn't happen that way, it's the trainer's fault! Because of this attitude, they fail to acknowledge the connection of the learning partnership that is required between trainer and student. In plain English, they fail to take ownership!

End of Social Commentary!
What About The Trainers Role?

Secondly, trainers often fail to integrate ownership into the classroom process, elevating the problem to a new level. Students sit in the classroom and wonder, "When is this lady going to teach me something," while the *instructor* is asking, "Why aren't these people more involved?"

What Does Participant Ownership Look Like In The Classroom?

We ask this question because, as trainers, we would like to get an "ownership-at-a-glance" reading on the students. Although we cannot read their mind (yet), we can look for specific behaviors that are indications of the level of ownership students are accepting. Classic signs of a student accepting ownership include: participation in discussions, asking questions, and volunteering for class assignments, such as table leader, timekeeper, etc. In other words, a student's level of ownership can be quickly assessed by observing their level of *involvement*.

Who Really "Owns" The Ownership Issue?

As I said, ownership is a shared responsibility. However, as the previous scenario illustrates, you will quickly find yourself in a learning stalemate of sorts if one party does not take the initiative to begin the ownership process. Remember in Chapter 3 when we said that classroom leadership is both a privilege and a responsibility? This is the responsibility part. In our role as trainers and tour guides to learning, we must accept responsibly to provide methods that encourage and nurture ownership in the classroom. My experience is that 98% of people respond favorably to these methods. The 2% that don't get it, are really the 2% who don't <u>want</u> to get it. (It's an attitude thing.) Focus your efforts on the 98% who are receptive, and, who knows? Maybe some of the 2% will wake up and follow along!

But What Does It Cost?

The following methods are easy to apply, require minimum (if any) monetary investment, and are proven to engage your participants in the learning process. Notice that each method requires the trainer to act as the tour guide, or facilitator, while the students take ownership by identifying and solving problems. The students make the decisions. The tour guide simply leads them in the right direction, making sure they don't get lost during the tour!

Four Classroom Ownership Methods That Get Students Involved!

Ownership Method: Start Your Engines

As class begins, divide participants into small teams of 3-5. Allow each team to pick a leader. The leader will be responsible to lead their team in discussions and assist you in keeping the participants focused throughout the day. Look for some effective examples of table team development in Chapter 5, utilizing the S.L.A.M. method. *Benefit: Get participants involved from the very start of the class.*

Ownership Method: The "Three In Three" Activity

This activity will jumpstart the ownership expectation. It is a great method to use at the beginning of any class. Allow 3 minutes for teams to list the top 3 things they hope to bring back to their job by <u>attending and participating</u> in

this class. Keep these expectations posted on a flipchart paper throughout the day. Near the end of class, circle back to the expectations. Were they: missed, met, or exceeded?
Benefit: Participants establish immediate learning expectations.

Ownership Method: The Great Debate

This is an effective closing activity. Divide the class into two teams. Each team is allowed 5 minutes to identify the top 5 obstacles students will face as they attempt to apply their new knowledge back on the job. The teams switch lists and then determine specific actions that can be taken to overcome the identified challenges to make the training work. Allow 5 minutes for each team to present their ideas. Finally, the tour guide facilitates an open discussion that will result in the identification of specific things that must happen in order for the training to work back on the job. The students will leave class feeling confident and prepared to face the obstacles that lie ahead.

Benefit: Provide clear direction on practical application methods.

Ownership Method: Sponsor a Learning Reunion

This activity provides a process for the participants to have a "learning reunion" 30, 60, or 90 days after class. During the reunion, students reflect on the class they attended, discussing what worked and what didn't, while sharing ideas and insights with each other. You can incorporate fun themes such as an ice cream social and ask everyone to bring their favorite ice cream to the class reunion.
Benefit: Continued learning through follow-up and networking.

The Bottom Line About Participant Ownership

Ownership in the classroom is a shared responsibility between the tour guide and the student. It is the responsibility of the tour guide to establish methods and processes that will make participant ownership a reality. During class, a student's level of ownership can be quickly assessed by observing their level of *involvement*. After class, the true measure of whether or not students accepted ownership for their learning experience is the level of execution or the application of their new knowledge. *Good trainers* may know this, but **Great Trainers make it happen!**

Chapter 5
Give a S.L.A.M. To Your Students!

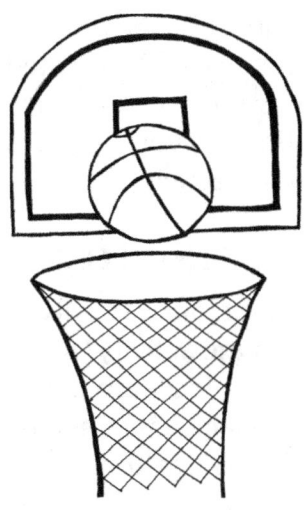

What Is S.L.A.M.?

S.L.A.M. is a **S**upportive **L**earning **A**ctivity or **M**ethod. Many good trainers with the best intentions are skeptical of both the appropriateness and the value of supportive learning activities and methods. Great Trainers, however, know that most people learn best through self-discovery, so they will develop activities that place the learner in a discovery situation. Then, acting as the tour guide, they lead the learner through the discovery process, doing what a tour guide does best: showing the students around the subject matter, answering questions, lending their expertise, and ultimately guiding them through specific methods of practical application. As stated in Chapter 1, *"The goal of training is universal in that, regardless of the topic, the final expectation is to change behavior back on the job. Period!"* A good **S.L.A.M.** will accomplish this goal!

Three Keys To A Great S.L.A.M.

Using a Supportive Learning Activity or Method in the classroom can indeed help accomplish the goal of changing behavior back on the job, but the prospects of that result will quickly fade if the activity is not executed properly. To ensure your students get the most out of their learning activities, follow these suggestions as you select, practice, and execute your supportive learning activities.

Select: Develop a Brief List of Objectives!

Before you begin the hunt for an activity, ask yourself: What will the students learn from the activity? Does it fit into the course objectives? How will you facilitate discussion to debrief the class? Also, be sure to select activities that fit the topic. I often see trainers utilizing activities that have absolutely nothing to do with the course objectives, leaving the students openly questioning the purpose. Just because an activity may be fun does not mean it will add value to the learning experience.

Practice: And Then Practice Again!

I've seen many a good activity lose impact simply because the trainer was unprepared. Do some dry runs prior to class, making sure you have all the supplies and props required. Review and practice your role in the general presentation and debriefing of the activity.

Execute: Debrief!

This is the self-discovery portion of the training, which we have already established as a critical step in the learning process. During the debriefing session of a Supportive Learning Activity, the tour guide will:

- **Lead the debriefing discussion by asking questions.** Talk less. Listen more.

- **Ask the students to provide examples** of how they can best use the lessons learned in real life settings, back on the job.
- **Expect and entertain the tough, real life questions.** Facilitate discussion among the students to gather opinions and new ideas that will resolve potential problems.
- **Keep the discussion focused** to ensure students understand both the material and the practical application methods that they (the students) have determined.

The following are two generic S.L.A.M.'s that work very well with any group and with any topic. They require no expense or supplies, other than flipchart paper and markers. When facilitated properly, they will generate a lot of table discussion, increasing the participation level, and will cause all students to feel they are part of the class, not an observer. Each one may be facilitated in 20 minutes or less. As with most group activities, the selection of a table leader who has the desire and capacity to lead discussions is a key element to the success of the S.L.A.M. You can find more S.L.A.M.'s through the different resources listed on page number 81 of this book.

What's Going On In Your World?

This "front end/back end" Supportive Learning Activity is conducted as a pre-class assignment, and then is debriefed near the end of class as a review and/or problem solving method.

Tour Guide Instructions

The Set Up: Create a 4 column flip chart that lists the top 5 things that can go wrong on the job that relate to class topics. The first column will contain the 5 things that can go wrong. The other three columns are for students to check *"Yes," "No" or "I'm not sure"* to signify if these are issues in their workplace. Prior to the start of class, students use colored dots to signify their response.

The Activity: Near the end of the training session, the trainer divides participants into small work groups and each group then selects a table leader. The assignment is to review the responses noted on the "What's Going On" flipchart and then, using knowledge gained in the class, determine practical solutions to the issues. Table leaders then present their questions and solutions to the entire group for further comment and discussion.

The Value: This activity generates a lot of discussion and provides the trainer with valuable information concerning what the students are experiencing in the workplace.

What's Your Big Question?

Sometimes participants have a burning question that they simply do not feel comfortable asking in a group setting; unless they can ask the question anonymously, which is exactly what this Supportive Learning Activity allows! This is a great activity to conduct mid-point in the training, when many questions are beginning to develop.

Tour Guide Instructions

The Set Up: Students are allowed 3 minutes to jot down their "big question" on a piece of paper. The participants fold the paper to hide the question. The trainer collects the folded papers containing the questions from each table and redistributes them to different tables. Participants select a table leader, who facilitates the remainder of the activity. At this point, allow teams 10 minutes to complete the assignment and 5 minutes to present.

The Activity: The table leader collects, reviews and writes the questions on a piece of flipchart paper. Then they guide their team in discussions of possible solutions to each question and records them on the flipchart below the corresponding questions. Table leaders then present their questions and solutions to the entire group for further group discussion.

The Value: Peers provide the solutions to questions. This creates the beginning of a peer network that can develop after class. Read more about networking in Chapter 6.

The Bottom Line About Supportive Learning Activities or Methods

Utilizing a Supportive Learning Activity or Method can be a very effective technique. A thoughtfully prepared, well-facilitated S.L.A.M. will instigate broad discussions that resolve problems, while promoting team building, partnerships and networking. It is also one of the most underutilized, misused methods attempted by unprepared trainers. By following the *Three Keys To A Great S.L.A.M.,* you can ensure the activities used in your classroom are both effective and value-added. This will lead to specific methods of practical application, thus achieving the ultimate goal of training - to change behavior back on the job! *Good trainers* may know this, but ***Great Trainers* make it happen!**

Chapter 6
Resources and Networking!

The class is almost over. What's next? A good tour guide will always provide students with two important follow-up elements: resources (where can I go for additional information?) and networking opportunities (who can I call for help?).

Resource Objective:

Show students where to go for additional information after the class.

Here are five examples of methods you can use to provide on-going resources for your students.

Set Up a Resource Table

Stock it with handouts, books, magazine articles, and web site addresses that tie into class topics. Students love to graze the resource table during breaks and lunches. These materials can offer alternative sources of information for continued research.

Ask the Expert – The Student!

Students often have great contact information to share when it comes to resources that are available. Make time during the class to allow students to share their ideas with each other. Have a scribe take notes, then copy and distribute to participants at the end of the day.

Ask The Other Expert - The Tour Guide!

As the trainer, you should make yourself available to students after the class. Provide your business card with your phone number and email address to all participants. Make a point of conducting random contacts 2 weeks after the class to solicit feedback on the course, and to see how the students are using what they have learned. This information can be valuable when planning your next class!

Publish a Resource List and Talk About It!

Most organizations have people and departments that are excellent resources, but many times students don't know they are available or even exist! Develop a one page list of: 1) People 2) Departments and 3) Outside Resources. And don't just dump them on the handout table: talk about them! Take a few minutes to go through the list with the students. Better yet, invite someone who is on the list to speak for 10 minutes and allow <u>them</u> to review the resource list with your class!

Publish an After-Class Follow Up Email!

Two weeks after class, send an email to the participants with links to websites that provide additional outside information, support, or other course-related items of interest.

Networking Objective:

To provide avenues for students that lead to assistance, coaching or mentoring.

Here are three examples of networking opportunities that a trainer can create for students before, during, and after class.

Prior To Training: Play The Card Game!

Purchase 2 decks of playing cards. Select matching cards (2 king of hearts, etc.) and send out each card with a letter of instruction to participants in advance of class. In your letter, ask students to arrive 15 minutes early to meet their match - the other person who will be holding the same card as they are! Also in the letter you can list specific networking questions that they should ask each other when they meet. On training day, students walk through the door to your classroom and search for the holder of their matching card. When they meet, they both exchange information from the questions you included in the letter.

During Class Time: Take A Step Forward!

This is a great breakout activity that helps people get to know each other on a more personal level. It also gets people out of their chairs and on their feet! All participants are provided with a 3x5 card and are asked to jot down one exceptional or unusual thing that no one would commonly know about

them. For example, "I lived in France" or "I play concert piano." The cards are then collected by the trainer and placed in a hat (or box, whatever you have available). Participants are then asked to stand in a circle. The trainer draws a card from the hat and reads it aloud. Participants get 20 seconds to try to guess who wrote the card. After 20 seconds, the trainer asks the person who wrote the card to "step forward" into the circle to provide more detail about their experience.

At The Close Of Training:
Network Partner, Please Call Me!

This activity will establish a personal contact for each participant after the class. Students will enjoy the anticipation of a follow-up call by a fellow classmate.

Prior to this activity, collect email and snail-mail addresses from all students. To begin the activity, ask each participant to write a brief note, addressed to *"Dear Network Partner."* In the letter, the student should outline what they expect to be doing differently as a result of the training they have just completed. At the end of the letter, it should read: *"Please call or email me when you receive this letter so that we can discuss my progress. My contact information is…."* The trainer collects the letters, and mails them out at random two weeks after the training session ends.

The Bottom Line About Resources
and Networking In The Classroom

Students sometimes exit the classroom feeling overwhelmed with information. In post-course evaluations, students often request reliable resources for future use and more networking opportunities (i.e. they need to know where to go for additional information and who to call for help). The trainer owns this responsibility. By utilizing the resource and networking activities found in Chapter 6, you will deliver an on-going support process that extends learning beyond the classroom. *Good trainers* may know this, but ***Great Trainers*** **make it happen!**

Chapter 7
Bringing It All Together:
The Fusion Review Method

Should I Plan A Review? YES!

Many trainers associate a review only with courses that require written examination, seeing little or no value in conducting a review of other material. But, if we are after great retention (which we are) so people will apply their knowledge back on the job (which we want), conducting a great review is imperative to achieving these results. It is common knowledge that most people learn best through repetition. It is also widely accepted that most people remember more of what they experienced most recently. Therefore, it only makes sense that we provide a thorough review of the material at the end of the training day! Although review methods vary, I'd like to recommend one in particular that is a sure winner.

Which Method Of Review Yields The Best Results?

Which review method causes people to retain the most information? Actually, there is not one answer to that question. Some people learn best through repetition, while others learn by participating in activity and discussion. Still others learn through review testing or questioning. To satisfy all of these unique learning styles, I have developed a review process called "The Fusion Review."

What Is the Fusion Review?

As the name implies, the Fusion Review brings all styles of learning together into one process. When teaching an audience that is a mix of educational levels, the Fusion Review is most effective because you can design it to touch on every style of learning that may be present. Although designed to be the "final" review format for a training class, you can also design a Fusion Review and use parts of it as smaller sectional reviews throughout the day. Both methods have proven to be very effective, and in some cases, even entertaining! The Fusion Review is also very effective when preparing students for an examination that is scheduled at the conclusion of a classroom training session.

Preparing Your Fusion Review

There are three important steps to follow when preparing a review for your class:

1) Based on the course material, **determine the most important points of the training** that students must recall and use back on the job. This may include the building blocks of procedural steps, processes, policy, etc.
2) **Consider the amount of time available for review.** A good rule of thumb is to allow 1 hour of review for every 7 hours of instruction. If preparing students for an examination at the end of a course, consider scheduling 1

hour of review for every 5 hours of instruction.

3) Finally, **determine the elements of the Fusion Review that are best suited for your audience.** As mentioned earlier, if the audience has a broad mix of educational levels, using 4 or more different elements of review will touch on everyone's learning style. If your audience consists of engineers, a combination of testing and problem solving activities may be most effective. In contrast, for a group of retail managers who are accustomed to high levels of energy and interaction on the job, a series of competitive review activities may be just the ticket.

Examples of Elements You Can Add To A Fusion Review

Multiple Choice Quiz (Analytical)
There are 3 basic guidelines to follow when creating a multiple choice quiz:
1) It should contain no more than 20 questions
2) Every question should only have one correct answer
3) Please, no trick questions. You may also consider developing several short (5-10 questions) topical quizzes to use throughout the training session.

Flash Cards (Memorization)
Develop several decks of flash cards by topic (3x5 cards work well). On each card, post a question on one side, and the answer on the other side. Hand out one deck (or topic) per team. Allow students to quiz each other in their respective teams. Rotate the decks from team to team until all cards have been reviewed by all teams.

Case Studies (Interaction, Problem Solving, Analytical)
Group discussion is a key element in the use of case studies. By their very design, case studies can generate

a great amount of discussion and exploration. They are simple to execute: distribute handout, discuss in small teams, conduct a debriefing with the entire group, and then discuss the application of principles.

Interactive Video (Visual)

The key word here is "interactive." Do not be afraid to stop the video to facilitate discussions, ask questions, or make a point. When you get people involved in what they are visually experiencing, you will open a new door to ownership!

Keynote Review (Interaction)

In working teams, allow 15 minutes for the students to review their notes to determine the most important points of the course. First, students discuss their notes and come to a consensus of the main points. Next, they document the key points on a flip chart. Finally, they present their findings to the rest of the class. Talk about learning through repetition!

Notice that "games" are not mentioned as one of my favorite Fusion Review methods. Although games can be used as a form of review, my experience has been that people get too caught up in winning and losing the game, and what they *really* lose is a focus on learning the material. Games do have a place in the learning process, but not in the final review.

The Bottom Line About Course Reviews

Reviews are important because they anchor key points, which the learner will need back on the job. The Fusion Review method further anchors the information to the participant by "fusing" all the methods of learning together into one review process. It is effective because the trainer can design the review to touch on every style of learning that may be present in the audience. Fusion Reviews can be easily developed by following the 3 steps outlined in Chapter 7 under *Preparing Your Fusion Review*. *Good trainers* may know this, but ***Great Trainers* make it happen!**

Chapter 8
A Great Trainer Challenge:
"Make It Happen" in 60 minutes!

Has This Ever Happened To You?

There is an all-too-common dilemma faced by trainers today, and it goes something like this: You are assigned the task of conducting a 1-hour training session. Due to the obvious time constraint, the challenge is to successfully condense the message, maintain clarity, and engage participants in the learning process. If this scenario sounds familiar, read on! Utilizing Great Trainer techniques, you can "Make It Happen" in any 60-minute training situation by following a few simple steps.

Step One: *Define and Clarify the Message*

The first instinct of an *instructor* is to cram as much information as possible into one hour, hoping some of it will "stick" back on the job. A Great Trainer, on the other hand, realizes the purpose of training is to change behavior. The only way to accomplish this in the confines of one hour is to first define, and then clarify, the key learning points of the message. Key learning points, also referred to as the *Need-to-Know* points of the message, are considered to be those things that if executed, will cause behavior to change back on the job. If behavior has changed, learning has occurred and the training was a success. To define and clarify the message, begin by determining the Top 3 *Need-to-Know* points of your training presentation.

- Gather and review all the information relevant to your training session. This will include training guides, charts, handouts, reference materials, etc.

- On a separate piece of paper, create a simple two-column chart. Title one column *"Need-to-Know"* and the second column *"Nice-to-Know."*

- In the first column, list all the *Need-to-Know* topics of your training presentation. You can usually break them down into the top 3 actionable items that when executed correctly, will result in the desired behavioral change. Ask yourself: "When the participants leave the training room and return to work, what 3 things do I want them to do differently?" The answer to this question will help you create the *Need-to-Know* list, which will then develop into the central focus of your training presentation.

- In the second column, list all the *Nice-to-Know* topics. *Nice-to-Know* topics are considered an enhancement to the Top 3 *Need-to-Knows*, but <u>are not critical to the execution of the new task or behavior change</u>. Information deemed as *Nice-to-Know* is still valuable and should be used to <u>complement</u> the *Need-to-Know* topics. Utilize the *Nice-to-Know* information in the form of handouts, resource lists, or FYI slides that flash on the screen before class begins.

- Once complete, this simple chart displays the essence of the training presentation. Allow approximately 30 minutes for presentation of the *Need-to-Know* topics, and 30 minutes for review, discussion, and a question/answer session.

Step Two: *Create The Review*

In this situation, it is unlikely you will have time to conduct a supportive learning activity. After 30 minutes of presentation, the remaining time should be allocated for discussion of how to execute and/or apply learning and a brief question/answer session. Consider using one of the <u>Fusion Review Methods</u> suggested in Chapter 7 to anchor your presentation topics while gaining participation from the group. Be sure to choose an activity that is right for your audience. In this 60-minute situation, I would suggest creating a Keynote Review (Chapter 7-Fusion Review Methods) followed by a brief question/answer session.

Step Three: *Create a 360° Closing*

In a brief training presentation such as this, you'll want to close with a summation of the Top 3 *Need-to-Know* points. That's right, you are going to close with the same information you began with! Why? Studies indicate that people experience the best recall of information during two points of any presentation: the beginning and the end. By *ending* the presentation with a review of the *beginning*, you will dramatically improve the recall of the *Need-to-Know* points of the message, increasing the likelihood of application back on the job.

Step Four: *Provide Post-Training Resources*

Sometimes verbally, and always silently, the question *"Where can I go for help?"* will be asked by everyone in the room. Students need to know where to go for additional help and assistance after the training session. Review suggestions in Chapter 6, Resources and Networking.

You're done! By following these simple steps, you have created an effective training presentation with a clear message that can be delivered in a short period of time. Next, by utilizing the principles of creating a positive physical and emotional learning environment, you will greatly enhance the learning experience.

Manage the Physical Learning Environment, And Prepare the Emotional Learning Environment!

It is possible that you will have little control over certain aspects of the physical learning environment. For example, as an outside consultant, you may conduct short training seminars for clients. Although the location, time, and agenda may be pre-determined, remember that as a Great Trainer, you still own *some* aspects of the physical learning environment, and *nearly all* aspects of the emotional learning environment. Here are a few basic tips for our 60-minute training session example.

Prior to The Day of Training

When possible, schedule a walk-through of the facility. If issues with lighting, seating, or cleanliness are evident (top 3 distractions), you'll have some time to work with your client to make the needed improvements. Of course, if you are in a position to make those decisions, insist on the standards outlined in Chapter 1. If a physical walk-through is not possible, communicate your expectations to the proper authority in advance.

On The Day of Training

Arrive to the location at least 30-45 minutes early to set up the room. Show some hospitality! A good rule of thumb for even the shortest training presentation is to have some candy available for the participants to munch on and, at the very least, some water to wash it down with. Consider your participants as *guests* in your training session. Most of us would not consider inviting guests into our home without offering them something to drink or a snack. The same basic hospitality rule applies here. Most people expect this hospitality and, certainly, everyone will appreciate it!

As Participants Arrive For Training

Establish a positive emotional tone right from the start by greeting each participant as they enter the room. Review and use the steps of **WACCO**, outlined in Chapter 2.

Summary

A Great Trainer <u>Can</u> Make It Happen In 60 Minutes!

1.   **Make your presentation clear and concise** by focusing on the Top 3 *Need-to-Know* topics and saving the *Nice-to-Know* items for handouts and other supporting material.

2. **Create a learning review activity** to keep the audience engaged. Encourage discussion, get answers to questions, and make the learning experience fun.

3. **Use a 360° closer** to increase retention and ensure application back on the job.

4. **Make resources available** that will provide avenues of assistance when participants have questions or need clarification after the class.

5. **Establish a positive physical learning environment** by ensuring the room is clean, bright, and alive with both visual and audio activity. Use posters, pictures, pre-class slideshows and background music to reflect the theme of the training while adding an element of fun and curiosity to the event. Arrange tables to include notepads, pens, name tents, snacks, and water to create a welcoming tone to your presentation.

6. **Set a positive emotional tone** by greeting all participants as they enter the room. Make everyone feel welcome, comfortable, and relaxed.

The Bottom Line About Making It Happen In 60 Minutes

Whether you're facilitating a 60-minute training session or a 5-day course, the techniques found in this book can be applied to any training situation. By identifying the *Need-to-Know* points of information, you can define and clarify the message to make it fit into any timeframe. An abbreviated Fusion Review combined with a 360° closer, will dramatically improve recall of the *Need-to-Know* message, increasing the probability of on-the-job application. Moreover, by providing post-training resources, participants will leave the training session feeling more confident knowing "where to go" for additional assistance. *Good trainers* may know this, but **Great Trainers make it happen!**

Chapter 9
Designing a Short Presentation
The Great Trainer Way!

When you are scheduled to give a short presentation to an important audience, do you feel a bit nervous? That's O.K.! A little nervousness is actually a positive sign that you care about your audience, your message, and your results!

In addition to utilizing many of the steps outlined in the previous chapters, you can plan and execute a great presentation using the **Presentation Planning Guide**. Using this template, you can plan, develop, and deliver a great presentation that will be a rewarding experience for both you and your audience!

Why Presentations Fail

First of all, when I say a presentation has failed, what do I mean? Simply that the content was not well received, used, or retained by the audience. Many of us have had the opportunity to sit though presentations that were less-than-inspiring, lacking in useful information, or just downright boring. I believe there are four main causes to a presentation failure:

1) **The presenter is unprepared.** This causes the audience to ask, *"Does this person really know what they are talking about?"*
2) The communication of ideas and/or **information is incomplete**. This causes the audience to ask for clarifications, often to the point of distraction.
3) **Too much detail is provided** – details that have little to do with the main objective. It leaves the audience asking, *"Can you please just get to the point?"*
4) **The presenter greatly exceeds the allotted amount of time**, which causes the audience to ask, *"When will this end?"*

Follow the simple steps in this Presentation Planning Guide to see the quality of your presentations immediately improve!

The Presentation Planning Guide

Step 1: Plan the Presentation

Duration: Be a Conscientious Speaker – Begin and End On Time

Determine the amount of time you are allowed to speak. As you create your presentation, be certain to schedule <u>less time</u> than you are given. Ending early will be perceived as a show of respect for other people's time. If your presentation extends beyond the allotted amount of time, the audience may break out the tomatoes - and they won't be for eating! Another tip: find out who is scheduled to speak before you. If that person is the messenger of bad news, or they far exceed their time allotment, it may be appropriate to call for a short break before you take center stage. This will help the audience clear their minds and focus on your presentation, rather than dealing with leftover distractions caused by the previous speaker.

Audience: Know Who They Are, and What They Expect

One reason so many presentations fall flat is due to the failure of the presenter knowing and understanding the needs and expectations of the audience. Do your homework ahead of time. How many people are attending? What is their motivation to listen to you? What is going on in their "work world" that may affect their attitude towards your presentation?

Objectives: Define the Top 3 *Need-to-Know* Topics

What are the three most important points you want the audience to recall? What behavior do you want to change?

Step 2: Develop the Presentation Outline

Opening

The opening segment of the presentation should grab the attention of the audience, but remember that it must have some relevance to the main topic. The opening statement or activity should complement the main points of the message. Using awkward activities or stories that do not fit, leave people wondering *"What's your point?"* Avoid preaching, complaining or delivering bad news during the opening. Doing so will result in a mental shut-down of the audience. Using a short, well-defined opening activity, story, or statement can have the audience hanging on your every word, and talking about your presentation for weeks to come! See my *Recommended Resources* page for books that offer great opening and closing activities.

Talking Points

Be specific. Keep the main message of the presentation short and to-the-point. Script the *Need-to-Know* topics and save the *Nice-to-Know* information for handouts. Use short illustrations, and be sure to keep them positive. If using stories, jokes, or quotations, be certain they are appropriate – rated "G" for general audiences. Stay away from jokes or statements regarding sex, politics, or religion.

Closing

This is your opportunity to sum up the main message and to give the audience their marching orders. *"In summary, I'd like you to remember these three points ..."* Ask for questions, but do it in a way that <u>encourages</u> participants to ask them, such as: *"What questions do you have?"* rather than the standard - *"Any questions?"*

Step 3: Deliver the Presentation!

Be prepared!

Practice your presentation. Anticipate the tough questions and practice your responses. And don't forget to look your best! Dress one notch up from the dress code of the audience.

During Your Presentation

Speak loudly and distinctly. It's important that you act and speak with confidence. Maintain good eye contact. As you are speaking, look directly at one person for about 5 seconds, then on to the next person for 5 seconds, and so on. Particularly effective in small groups, this technique will cause people to feel as though you are speaking <u>directly to them</u>. Another tip: Do not overuse distracting hand gestures.

The Bottom Line About Designing Short Presentations

To use the Presentation Planning Guide format to structure your presentation, start by conducting some research on the audience. Once you understand the needs and expectations of the audience, you can develop the body of your presentation into the Top 3 *Need-to-Know* topics. Anticipate the tough questions and be prepared with answers. Finally, practice your presentation several times to ensure you deliver the message with confidence. *Good trainers* may know this, but **Great Trainers make it happen!**

Chapter 10
Review: Great Trainer Highlights

Let's review the key points of *Great Trainers Make It Happen!*

Chapter 1
The Physical Learning Environment

Creating an inviting physical environment is the first critical step in the delivery of any successful training session. Keeping participants comfortable in a clean, spacious, well-lit, well-ventilated room with comfortable chairs and refreshments will keep them focused on the topics at hand. And keeping them focused is what leads to learning, retention, and on-the-job application.

Chapter 2
The Emotional Learning Environment

Equally as important is the <u>emotional tone</u> you establish in your classroom. The moment a participant enters the training room *"The emotional tone is set in stone"* for the remainder of the class. You can create and manage the emotional learning environment by making the classroom come alive with activity and color before the class begins! This will create a welcoming environment for your students and cause participation to increase, expectations to rise, and attention levels to soar.

Chapter 3
Classroom Leadership–Become a "Tour Guide" to Learning!

Acting as a "tour guide" will help you become a more effective trainer and will cause adult learners to return to the workplace *excited* to put their new knowledge to work. Utilizing tour guide techniques will make your class anything-but-ordinary, causing people to actually look forward to your next event! Finally, remember that classroom leadership is both a privilege and a responsibility; display that belief through your actions every day!

Chapter 4

Participant Ownership

Ownership in the classroom is a shared responsibility between the tour guide and the student. It is the responsibility of the tour guide to establish methods and processes that will make participant ownership a reality. During class, a student's level of ownership can be quickly assessed by observing their level of *involvement*. After class, the true measure of whether or not students accepted ownership for their learning experience is the level of execution or the application of their new knowledge.

Chapter 5

Give a S.L.A.M. To Your Students!

Utilizing a Supportive Learning Activity or Method can be a very effective technique. A thoughtfully prepared, well-facilitated S.L.A.M. will instigate broad discussions that resolve problems, while promoting team building, partnerships and networking. It is also one of the most underutilized, misused methods attempted by unprepared trainers. By following the *Three Keys To A Great S.L.A.M.*, you can ensure the activities used in your classroom are both effective and value-added, which will lead to specific methods of practical application, thus achieving the ultimate goal of training - to change behavior back on the job!

Chapter 6

Networking and Resources

Students sometimes exit the classroom feeling overwhelmed with information. In post-course evaluations, students often request reliable resources for future use and more networking opportunities (i.e. they need to know where to go for additional information, and who to call for help). The trainer owns this responsibility. By utilizing the resource and networking activities found in Chapter 6, you will deliver an on-going support process that extends learning beyond the classroom.

Chapter 7

Bringing It All Together: The Fusion Review Method

Reviews are important because they anchor key points, which the learner will need back on the job. The Fusion Review method further anchors the learning by "fusing" all the methods of learning together into one review process. It is effective because the trainer can design the review to touch on every style of learning that may be present in the audience. Fusion Reviews can be easily developed by following the 3 steps outlined in Chapter 7 under *Preparing Your Fusion Review*.

Chapter 8

Making It Happen In 60 Minutes!

Whether you're facilitating a 60-minute training session or a 5-day course, the techniques found in this book can be applied to any training situation. By identifying the *Need-to-Know* points of information, you can define and clarify the message to make it fit into any timeframe. An abbreviated Fusion Review combined with a 360° closer, will dramatically improve recall of the *Need-to-Know* message, increasing the probability of on-the-job application. Moreover, by providing post-training resources, participants will leave the training session feeling more confident knowing "where to go" for additional assistance.

Chapter 9

Designing Short Presentations
The Great Trainer Way!

To use the Presentation Planning Guide format to structure your presentation, start by conducting some research on the audience. Once you understand the needs and expectations of the audience, you can develop the body of your presentation into the Top 3 *Need-to-Know* topics. Anticipate the tough questions and be prepared with answers. Finally, practice your presentation several times to ensure you deliver the message with confidence.

Good trainers may know this, but **Great Trainers make it happen!**

The Final Word

Students Have Expectations

Everyone who attends a training seminar has certain expectations, such as:

- The trainer will be knowledgeable of the topic
- Class will be held in a clean, comfortable, and safe environment
- I can ask questions, and I'll get answers
- I'll gain new knowledge that will help me do my job better
- If I can have some fun in all of this, it's a huge "plus"

The purpose of this book is to provide methods that will meet, and in most cases exceed, these expectations.

It Seems Like A Lot Of Extra Work. Why Bother?

A fair question, asked by many trainers as they begin their *Great Trainer* journey. I found the answer in a popular book, <u>A Passion For Excellence</u> by Tom Peters and Nancy Austin. In one chapter, the authors discuss the true meaning of "coaching," as it should be applied in today's business environment. As you read the following excerpt, think about substituting the word "training" for the word "coaching."

"Coaching (Training) <u>is not</u> about memorizing techniques or devising the perfect game plan. It's about really paying attention to people - really believing in them, really caring about them, really involving them."

If you aspire to be a great trainer, you will <u>make the time</u> to deliver training that is both participant-centered and engaging, because you care enough to believe in the potential of the students by *involving* them in their learning process.

It's Your Choice

Whether you make the learning experience energizing or boring, inspiring or forgettable, as the classroom leader, you will leave your mark on each participant's life and livelihood. Having a choice, wouldn't you prefer to make it a *positive* experience, one that will be remembered for years to come?

A Training Acorn

Many years ago, my parents lived in a house that was located on a heavily wooded lot filled with huge oak trees. Although beautiful, they often produced thousands of acorns that would litter the driveway and garage. One afternoon, while visiting with my wife and daughters, my stepfather asked if I would sweep out the garage, as the acorns were beginning to pile up. So I began the task, sweeping up acorns into a dust pan and dumping them into an old trash barrel in the back of the garage.

I was about half-way through the job, when all of a sudden, I heard my youngest daughter, Cara, who was 5 years old at the time, scream in her highest high-pitched voice: ***"Dad!"*** It was one of those screams that will catch a parent's attention - if you are a parent, you know the sound. Anyway, I stopped sweeping and turned around to find her staring at me with the most astonished look on her face. That *"what-the-heck-are-you-doing?!"* look only a five-year-old can give. Startled, I asked "What…what's wrong?" Cara stared back, eyes glaring. It was clear that I was in *big* trouble. "What are you doing?!" she shouted. "Nothing, just sweeping up these acorns," I replied. "But, Dad, you're throwing them away!" "So what?" I said, as I continued sweeping. Then my five-year-old daughter said something that has stuck with me for nearly two decades. She said:

"In school I learned that if you plant acorns in the ground they will grow into trees. Throwing away an acorn is like throwing away a tree. Let's plant one instead, and watch it grow."

In many respects, this book is your training acorn. You have a choice of what you can do with it. You can toss it away **or** you can use it to plant some ideas. Ideas that, when nurtured, will enhance your training skills and guide you in your journey to become the Great Trainer you want to be.

It is my hope that you will chose to plant this acorn.
Be a *Great Trainer* and make it happen!

Questions, Answers, and Solutions

Q: This is a lot of stuff to remember! Any suggestions on how I can condense the information for easy review?
A: Yes! Turn to page 84 for a copy of The Great Trainer's Checklist.

Q: I conduct training for clients who provide training rooms that are already set up, not always in the best fashion. What can I do about it?
A: Remember, **Great Trainers make it happen!** Get to the training site a day early to scout out the facility, seating arrangements, lighting, etc. At the very least, you can rearrange the seating layout to fit your training needs. Don't simply accept things as they are. Make it happen!

Q: What is the ideal training room set up?
A: Actually, the ideal room arrangement depends on what type of training you are conducting. If you are looking for moderate to high levels of group participation and interaction, I recommend the classroom arrangement illustrated on page 83. Using this interactive model, you can actually create small workgroups within a larger workgroup.

Q: Student introductions can sometimes be awkward and time consuming. What suggestions to you have to maintain time control while still allowing participants to have fun and learn a little about each other at the beginning of class?
A: Use the name tent exercise! See page 82 for instructions and an example. Allow the participants to share the information on their name tents as a method of introduction to their work group. This proves to be a quick, fun, process that is controlled by the tour guide to keep the agenda on schedule, while allowing participants to get to know each other.

Q: I am creating a small workshop and wish to structure it with Great Trainer techniques. What is a fast, easy-to-use method to do this?
A: Follow the steps outlined in Chapter 8. Next, consider using the 20-20-20 design method. Develop each hour of your workshop to allow for 20 minutes of instruction, 20 minutes of activity, and 20 minutes of application discussion. This simple instructional design method allows for participant-centered learning, group interaction, and most importantly, discussion of how to apply their new knowledge back on the job.

Got Training Questions?
I Have Answers!

Please send your questions and comments to:
ben.olson@cptrainer.net

For more *Great Trainer*
information visit my website:

www.cptrainer.net

Recommended Resources

Here are three top-notch organizations that can provide you with immediate assistance and resources in your quest to become a Great Trainer. I highly recommend each of these organizations. Go to their websites and check out all the great things they have to offer!

The Bob Pike Group
7620 W. 78th Street
Minneapolis, MN 55439
(800) 383-9210
www.BobPikeGroup.com

- *Train-The-Trainer Boot Camp*, a two-day seminar designed to dramatically improve the design and delivery of training programs
- *Creative Training Techniques Handbook, Third Edition* By Robert W. Pike, CSP, CPAE-Speakers Hall of Fame
  Tips, Tactics, and How-To's for Delivering Effective Training

- *Creative Training Techniques Newsletter*
  Subscription is available on their website.
  Awesome training tips collected from trainers around the world
- *The Best Of Creative Training Techniques Newsletter*
  Over 400 great ideas taken from articles published in the newsletter

Orion Training Company
14007 SE 28th Street
Vancouver, WA 98683
(360) 883-0610
www.trainingtreasures.com

- *Training Treasures Magazine*
  A leading publication of solid train-the-trainer content containing creative ideas and training techniques

The American Society for Training and Development (ASTD)
1640 King Street, Box 1443
Alexandria, VA 22313-2043
Phone: (703) 683-8100
www.ASTD.org

- ASTD (American Society for Training & Development) is the world's largest association dedicated to workplace learning and performance.
- A terrific website containing great resources for both new and experienced trainers.

Toys, games, quotations and animations can stimulate creativity and drive participant involvement to new levels! Here are some of my favorites:

Animation Web Sites
www.animationfactory.com
www.animationlibrary.com
www.bestanimations.com

Training Toys
www.trainerswarehouse.com
www.officeplayground.com

Quotations
www.quotationspage.com
www.quoteland.com
www.wisdomquotes.com

Games and Activities Books
These books are available on Amazon.com

The Big Book Of Humorous Training Games
By Doni Tamblyn and Sharyn Weiss

Quick Teambuilding Activities For Busy Managers
By Brian Cole Miller

101 Games For Trainers: A Collection Of The Best Activities From Creative Training Techniques Newsletter
By Bob Pike and Chris Busse

The Ten-Minute Trainer:
150 Ways To Teach It Quick And Make It Stick!
By Sharon L. Bowman and Dave Meier

Window Pane Name Tent
Student Introduction Activity

Instructions

With the paper provided, fold it into thirds, making a triangular name tent.

With markers provided at your table, write your first name on the front of the name tent. Feel free to color and get creative!

On the backside of the name tent (the side facing you), write or draw the following:

- In the upper-left corner, the name of the company you work for or your position.
- In the upper-right corner, list your favorite hobby or time-off activity.
- In the lower-left corner, list the first thing you would buy if you won the lottery.
- In the lower-right corner, the number of years you have worked in your field.

```
+-----------------------------------------------+
|                                               |
|            Benjamin                           |
|                                               |
+-----------------------------------------------+
```

```
+-----------------------------------------------+
|  Center Point Resources, LLC   Fishing, camping and  |
|           Owner                   playing guitar     |
|                                               |
|                                               |
|   A ranch in Montana          Nearly 40 years,  |
|  with horses, of course!     but who's counting? |
+-----------------------------------------------+
```

Interactive Classroom Arrangement

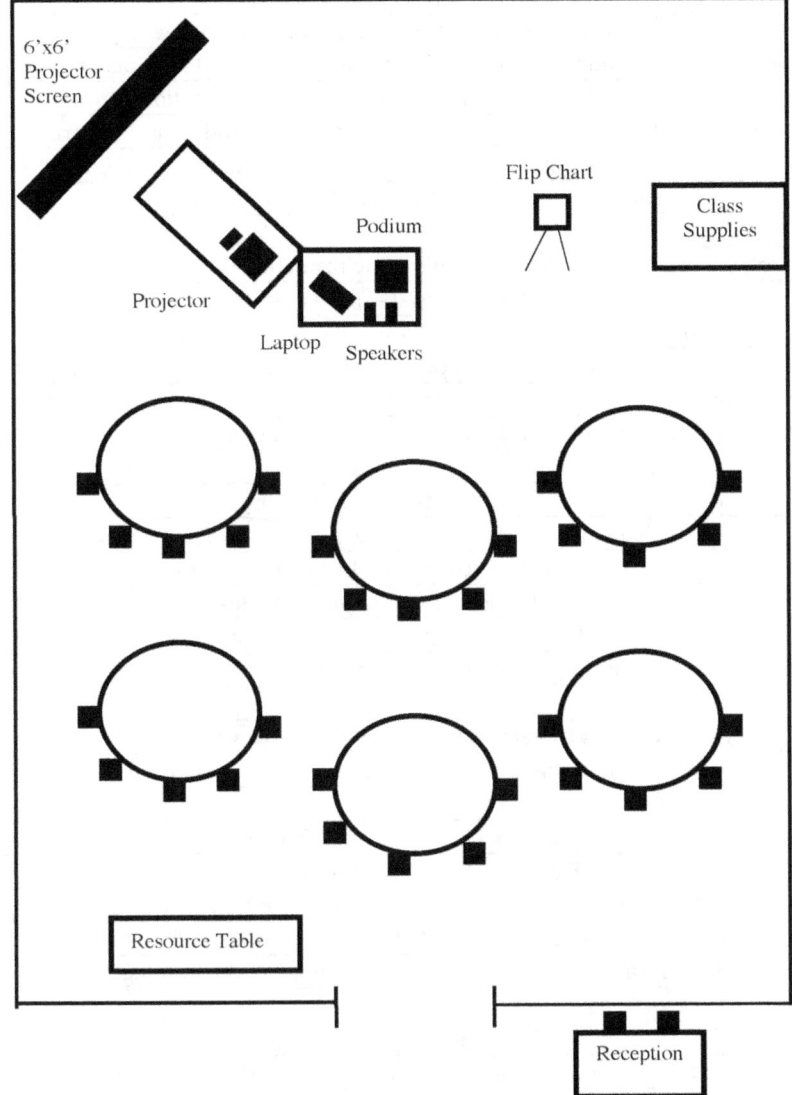

Great Trainer's Checklist

	Create a Positive Physical Learning Environment
	Training room size adequate for number of participants (800 sq. ft. per 20 students)
	Seating is arranged to benefit student interaction
	Room is bright, clean, with comfortable chairs - tables and chairs in good repair
	Ventilation controls available for adjustment to control heat/cooling
	Refreshments are available (at least a few light snacks and water)
	Create a Positive Emotional Learning Environment (Follow Steps of WACCO)
	Welcome each participant upon arrival – make them feel welcome and relaxed
	Action – background music, pre-class slides containing cartoons, quotes
	Create Curiosity – display props that tie in to the training topics
	Create Color – photographs, posters, table tents, post-it notes, pens, etc.
	Opportunity – take advantage of the opportunity and privilege of being a leader
	Be A Tour Guide To Learning
	Facilitate discussions – encourage questions and networking
	Allow students to come to their own conclusions
	Ask students for real life examples
	Focus on the practical application of what you are teaching
	Remain approachable before, during, and after the class
	Help Students Develop Ownership In Their Learning Experience
	Facilitate activities that involve students and engage them in the process
	Give a S.L.A.M. To Your Students
	Develop a brief list of class objectives
	Select Supportive Learning Activities and Methods that support objectives
	Practice your facilitation role – be prepared!
	Execute and then debrief the class to complete the learning cycle
	Provide Resources and Networking
	Utilize methods outlined in Chapter 6 to provide after-the-class resources
	Utilize a networking process that will lead to coaching and mentoring after class
	Prepare A Fusion Review
	Determine most important points of the training
	Consider amount of time available for review when selecting activities
	Select elements that are best suited for your audience

Make It Happen In 60 Minutes
Define and clarify your training message – identify the *Need-to-Know* topics
Create a review right for the audience to keep them involved and engaged
Develop a 360° closing message to increase retention
Provide post-training resources so the students know where to go for help

Words of Wisdom

This is a selection of my favorite sayings. Use them as a tie-in to the theme or topic of your training session prior to class, during breaks, or to stimulate discussion. Also, for websites that provide quotations on any topic, see my top 3 picks listed on the *Recommended Resources* page.

About Leadership
- *Leadership is a privilege. The people that truly believe this are the most effective leaders, teachers, mentors, coaches, and managers.*

About Success
- *The true measure of success lies not so much in what you have achieved, but in whether you have made a difference – it's knowing you have touched the lives of others, and have in some way made the world a little bit brighter, a little bit better.*

About Change
- *If you begin to change the way you look at things, the things you look at will begin to change.*

About People Who Constantly Disappoint You
- *When people show you who they are, believe them.*

About The Value of Training
- *Training is an investment. What goes around <u>really does</u> come around.*

About Speed Is Life

- *In today's business world, some say "Speed is Life." This is true; however, speed is worthless without accuracy. Slow down – do it right the first time.*

About Doing Things Right

- *If you don't have the time to do it right the first time, when will you have the time to do it over?*

About First Steps

- *Don't get discouraged during the first steps of a tough project. Remember that building the basement is always dirty work.*

About Life

- *Everything <u>really does</u> turn out alright in the end. If it's not alright, then it's not the end.*

About The Author

With 40 years of food service, retail management and training experience, Ben Olson has designed and delivered training courses that are focused on the learner – inspiring, engaging and fun! He has employed his **Great Trainer** techniques to Fortune 500 companies across the country, energizing audiences both large and small.

Ben is the founder and president of Center Point Resources, LLC, a food safety training company based in Illinois that provides **Great Trainer** techniques to clients throughout the United States.

Ben is an active member of a variety of organizations, including the American Society of Training and Development and the Illinois Environmental Health Association. He is also a licensed instructor with the National Registry of Food Safety Professionals, the National Restaurant Association Educational Foundation, and the Illinois Department of Public Health.

Ben is happily married to his wife, Shelby, and has three lovely daughters: Melissa, Lauren and Cara. When he's not busy being a **Great Trainer**, Ben enjoys model railroading, fishing and playing guitar.

www.ingramcontent.com/pod-product-compliance
Lightning Source LLC
Chambersburg PA
CBHW071245170526
45165CB00003B/1250